TODAY
I MANIFEST & CREATE THE LIFE I DESIRE

This 33x3 Challenge Workbook Belongs to:

Make it Happen Publishing Inc.

www.mihpublishing.com
Send all inquires to books@mihpublishing.com

THE LAW OF ATTRACTION TECHNIQUE: 33X3 CHALLENGE

WHAT TO DO:

Focus on one goal and write out a clear statement in the present tense (like you already have it and from a place of gratitude) that outlines what you desire. For 3 consecutive days you will write out this statement 33 times. Be sure to stay focused while you're writing your lines and be sure to complete all 33 lines during your daily session. At the end of the 3rd day, release your intention and trust that it will come!

(For example: "I am excited and thankful for the extra $10,000 in my bank account this month")

33X3 MANIFESTING CHALLENGE TIPS

- Use a Pen! Purple, blue or red are preferred.

- Prepare by getting into a relaxed state/mood. Ambient light or candles, soothing music etc.

- Remove any possible distractions and be mindful and present when writing your lines.

- Be clear and detailed about what you want to manifest. Keep it to one sentence.

- Including words of gratitude and emotions into your statement are essential!

- Be excited about what you are manifesting - Feel the emotions of receiving what you want.

- Work on only one goal at a time (for the consecutive 3 days) before moving to the next one.

- This is not homework and it should not feel bad to do. Get into a high vibrational space.

- Saying the words as you write them can help keep you focused.

- Visualize your life as you want it to be.

- Meditating before and after writing your daily lines is beneficial.

- DO NOT SKIP A DAY or SPLIT YOUR 33 LINES INTO DIFFERENT TIMES DURING THE DAY

- ALL 33 LINES MUST BE WRITTEN DURING ONE SESSION.

- At the end of 3 days - release your affirmation and trust that the Universe will bring it to you.

- When you've completed the 33X3 Challenge and have successfully manifested your goal, remember to record your success in this journal for future reference and confirmation.

- Be grateful for all that the Universe brings to you!

*** NOW GO AND GET STARTED ON MANIFESTING THE LIFE YOU WANT AND DESERVE! ***

MANIFESTATION INTENTION:

The partner I seek is also seeking me. I now release any blocks that are standing between us. I don't chase, I attract. What belongs to me will simply find me.

(In the present tense & a place of gratitude, write a clear statement of your intended manifestation as if you already have it)

1 The partner I seek is also seeking me. I now release any blocks that are standing between us.

2 The partner I seek is also seeking me. I now release any blocks that are standing between us.

3 The partner I seek is also seeking me. I now release any blocks that are standing between us.

4 The partner I seek is also seeking me. I now release any blocks that are standing between me us

5 The partner I seek is also seeking me. I now release any blocks that are standing between us.

6 The partner I seek is also seeking me. I now release any blocks that are standing between us.

7 The partner I seek is also seeking me. I now release any blocks that are standing between us.

8 The partner I seek is also seeking me. I now release any blocks that are standing between us.

9 The partner I seek is also seeking me. I now release any blocks that are standing between us.

10 The partner I seek is also seeking me. I now release any blocks that are standing between us.

11 The partner I seek is also seeking me. I now release any blocks that are standing between us.

12 The partner I seek is also seeking me. I now release any blocks that are standing between us.

13 The partner I seek is also seeking me. I now release any blocks that are standing between us.

14 The partner I seek is also seeking me. I now release any blocks that are standing between us.

15 The partner I seek is also seeking me. I now release any blocks that are standing between us.

16 The partner I seek is also seeking me. I now release any blocks that are standing between us.

17 The partner I seek is also seeking me. I now release any blocks that are standing between us.

18 The partner I seek is also seeking me. I now release any blocks that are standing between us.

19 The partner I seek is also seeking me. I now release any blocks that are standing between us.

20 The partner I seek is also seeking me. I now release any blocks that are standing between us.

21 The partner I seek is also seeking me. I now release any blocks that are standing between us.

22 The partner I seek is also seeking me. I now release any blocks that are standing between us.

23 The partner I seek is also seeking me. I now release any blocks that are standing between us.

24 The partner I seek is also seeking me. I now release any blocks that are standing between us.

25 The partner I seek is also seeking me. I now release any blocks that are standing between us.

26 The partner I seek is also seeking me. I now release any blocks that are standing between us.

27 The partner I seek is also seeking me. I now release any blocks that are standing between us.

28 The partner I seek is also seeking me. I now release any blocks that are standing between us.

29 The partner I seek is also seeking me. I now release any blocks that are standing between us.

30 The partner I seek is also seeking me. I now release any blocks that are standing between us.

31 The partner I seek is also seeking me. I now release any blocks that are standing between us.

32 The partner I seek is also seeking me. I now release any blocks that are standing between us.

33 The partner I seek is also seeking me. I now release any blocks that are standing between us.

MANIFESTATION MINDSET: Why do you desire this intention in your life?

I desire this intention because I welcome love into my life. I am worthy of love, loyalty and companionship. I give love to those that are in my life. I deserve to be loved for who I am. I am in a happy, loving and affectionate relationship.

(Get into the right mindset before you continue to write out the EXACT SAME manifestation intention from day 1 below)

1 The partner I seek is also seeking me. I now release any blocks that are standing between us.

2 The partner I seek is also seeking me. I now release any blocks that are standing between us.

3 The partner I seek is also seeking me. I now release any blocks that are standing between us.

4 The partner I seek is also seeking me. I now release any blocks that are standing between us.

5 The partner I seek is also seeking me. I now release any blocks that are standing between us.

6 The partner I seek is also seeking me. I now release any blocks that are standing between us.

7 The partner I seek is also seeking me. I now release any blocks that are standing between us.

8 The partner I seek is also seeking me. I now release any blocks that are standing between us.

9 The partner I seek is also seeking me. I now release any blocks that are standing between us.

10 The partner I seek is also seeking me. I now release any blocks that are standing between us.

11 The partner I seek is also seeking me. I now release any blocks that are standing between us.

12 The partner I seek is also seeking me. I now release any blocks that are standing between us.

13 The partner I seek is also seeking me. I now release any blocks that are standing between us.

14 The partner I seek is also seeking me. I now release any blocks that are standing between us.

15 The partner I seek is also seeking me. I now release any blocks that are standing between us.

16 The partner I seek is also seeking me. I now release any blocks that are standing between us.

17 The partner I seek is also seeking me. I now release any blocks that are standing between us

18 The partner I seek is also seeking me. I now release any blocks that are standing between us.

19 The partner I seek is also seeking me. I now release any blocks that are standing between us.

20 The partner I seek is also seeking me. I now release any blocks that are standing between us.

21 The partner I seek is also seeking me. I now release any blocks that are standing between us.

22 The partner I seek is also seeking me. I now release any blocks that are standing between us

23 The partner I seek is also seeking me. I now release any blocks that are standing between us.

24 The partner I seek is also seeking me. I now release any blocks that are standing between us.

25 The partner I seek is also seeking me. I now release any blocks that are standing between us.

26 The partner I seek is also seeking me. I now release any blocks that are standing between us.

27 The partner I seek is also seeking me. I now release any blocks that are standing between us.

28 The partner I seek is also seeking me. I now release any blocks that are standing between us.

29 The partner I seek is also seeking me. I now release any blocks that are standing between us.

30 The partner I seek is also seeking me. I now release any blocks that are standing between us.

31 The partner I seek is also seeking me. I now release any blocks that are standing between us.

32 The partner I seek is also seeking me. I now release any blocks that are standing between us.

33 The partner I seek is also seeking me. I now release any blocks that are standing between us.

I RELEASE MY INTENTION WITH GRATITUDE AND LOVE, Dawan

MANIFESTATION MINDSET: Why are you grateful to have this intention?

I am grateful because I am loved. Love is welcomed into my life. I am grateful for all the healthy, loving relationships in my life.

(Get into the right mindset before you continue to write out the EXACT SAME manifestation intention from day 1 below)

1 The partner I seek is also seeking me. I now release any blocks that are standing between us.

2 The partner I seek is also seeking me. I now release any blocks that are standing between us.

3 The partner I seek is also seeking me. I now release any blocks that are standing between us.

4 The partner I seek is also seeking me. I now release any blocks that are standing between us.

5 The partner I seek is also seeking me. I now release any blocks that are standing between us.

6 The partner I seek is also seeking me. I now release any blocks that are standing between us.

7 The partner I seek is also seeking me. I now release any blocks that are standing between us.

8 The partner I seek is also seeking me. I now release any blocks that are between them standing between us.

9 The partner I seek is also seeking me. I now release any blocks that are standing between us.

10 The partner I seek is also seeking me. I now release any blocks that are standing between us.

11 The partner I seek is also seeking me. I now release any blocks that are standing between us.

12 The partner I seek is also seeking me. I now release any blocks that are standing between us.

13 The partner I seek is also seeking me. I now release any blocks that are standing between us.

14 The partner I seek is also seeking me. I now release any blocks that are standing between us.

15 The partner I seek is also seeking me. I now release any blocks that are standing between us

16 The partner I seek is also seeking me. I now release any blocks that are standing between us.

17 The partner I seek is also seeking me. I now release any blocks that are standing between us.

18 The partner I seek is also seeking me. I now release any blocks that are standing between us.

19 The partner I seek is also seeking me. I now release any blocks that are standing between us

20 The partner I seek is also seeking me. I now release any blocks that are standing between us

21 The partner I seek is also seeking me. I now release any blocks that are standing between us.

22 The partner I seek is also seeking me. I now release any blocks that are standing between us.

23 The partner I seek is also seeking me. I now release any blocks that are standing between us.

24 The partner I seek is also seeking me. I now release any blocks that are standing between us.

25 The partner I seek is also seeking me. I now release any blocks that are standing between us.

26 The partner I seek is also seeking me. I now release any blocks that are standing between us.

27 The partner I seek is also seeking me. I now release any blocks that are standing between us.

28 The partner I seek is also seeking me. I now release any blocks that are standing between us.

29 The partner I seek is also seeking me. I now release any blocks that are standing between us.

30 The partner I seek is also seeking me. I now release any blocks that are standing between us.

31 The partner I seek is also seeking me. I now release any blocks that are standing between us.

32 The partner I seek is also seeking me. I now release any blocks that are standing between us

33 The partner I seek is also seeking me. I now release any blocks that are standing between us

I RELEASE MY INTENTION WITH GRATITUDE AND LOVE, Pawan.

MANIFESTED INTENTION:

The partner I seek is also seeking me. I now release any blocks that are standing between us. I don't chase, I attract. What belongs to me will simply find me.

(REWRITE THE EXACT SAME manifestation intention from day 1 above)

MANIFESTATION SUCCESS STORY

Use these pages to write, illustrate or attach photos, receipts, evidence or proof of your 33x3 Success Story. This will help to document your manifesting journey and minimize resistence to future manifestations and the Law of Attraction.

33X3 CHALLENGE COMPLETION

MANIFESTATION INTENTION:

I now draw good fortune my way, into every area of my reality.

(In the present tense & a place of gratitude, write a clear statement of your intended manifestation as if you already have it)

1 I now draw good fortune my way, into every area of my reality.

2 I now draw good fortune my way, into every area of my reality.

3 I now draw good fortune my way, into every area of my reality.

4 I now draw good fortune my way, into every area of my reality.

5 I now draw good fortune my way, into every area of my reality.

6 I now draw good fortune my way, into every area of my reality.

7 I now draw good fortune my way, into every area of my reality.

8 I now draw good fortune my way, into every area of my reality.

9 I now draw good fortune my way, into every area of my reality.

10 I now draw good fortune my way, into every area of my reality.

11 I now draw good fortune my way, into every area of my reality.

12 I now draw good fortune my way, into every area of my reality.

13 I now draw good fortune my way, into every area of my reality.

14 I now draw good fortune my way, into every area of my reality.

15 I now draw good fortune my way, into every area of my reality.

16 I now draw good fortune my way, into every area of my reality.

17 I now draw good fortune my way, into every area of my reality.

18 I now draw good fortune my way, into every area of my reality.

19 I now draw good fortune my way, into every area of my reality.

20 I now draw good fortune my way, into every area of my reality.

21 I now draw good fortune my way, into every area of my reality.

22 I now draw good fortune my way, into every area of my reality.

23 I now draw good fortune my way, into every area of my reality.

24 I now draw good fortune my way, into every area of my reality.

25 I now draw good fortune my way, into every area of my reality.

26 I now draw good fortune my way, into every area of my reality.

27 I now draw good fortune my way, into every area of my reality.

28 I now draw good fortune my way, into every area of my reality.

29 I now draw good fortune my way, into every area of my reality.

30 I now draw good fortune my way, into every area of my reality.

31 I now draw good fortune my way, into every area of my reality.

32 I now draw good fortune my way, into every area of my reality.

33 I now draw good fortune my way, into every area of my reality.

I RELEASE MY INTENTION WITH GRATITUDE AND LOVE, Dawan

MANIFESTATION MINDSET: Why do you desire this intention in your life?

I desire good fortune because I am worthy of living a life of abundance, prosperity and love. I am worthy of all that I have manifested.

(Get into the right mindset before you continue to write out the EXACT SAME manifestation intention from day 1 below)

1 I now draw good fortune my way, into every area of my reality.

2 I now draw good fortune my way, into every area of my reality.

3 I now draw good fortune my way, into every area of my reality.

4 I now draw good fortune my way, into every area of my reality.

5 I now draw good fortune my way, into every area of my reality.

6 I now draw good fortune my way, into every area of my reality.

7 I now draw good fortune my way, into every area of my reality.

8 I now draw good fortune my way, into every area of my reality.

9 I now draw good fortune my way, into every area of my reality.

10 I now draw good fortune my way, into every area of my reality.

11 I now draw good fortune my way, into every area of my reality.

12 I now draw good fortune my way, into every area of my reality.

13 I now draw good fortune my way, into every area of my reality.

14 I now draw good fortune my way, into every area of my reality.

15 I now draw good fortune my way, into every area of my reality.

16 I now draw good fortune my way,
into every area of my reality.
17 I now draw good fortune my way,
into every area of my reality.
18 I now draw good fortune my way,
into every area of my reality.
19 I now draw good fortune my way,
into every area of my reality.
20 I now draw good fortune my way,
into every area of my reality.
21 I now draw good fortune my way,
into every area of my reality.
22 I now draw good fortune my way,
into every area of my reality.
23 I now draw good fortune my way,
into every area of my reality.
24 I now draw good fortune my way,
into every area of my reality.
25 I now draw good fortune my way,
into every area of my reality.
26 I now draw good fortune my way,
into every area of my reality.
27 I now draw good fortune my way,
into every area of my reality.
28 I now draw good fortune my way,
into every area of my reality.
29 I now draw good fortune my way,
into every area of my reality.
30 I now draw good fortune my way,
into every area of my reality.
31 I now draw good fortune my way,
into every area of my reality.
32 I now draw good fortune my way,
into every area of my reality.
33 I now draw good fortune my way,
into every area of my reality.

I RELEASE MY INTENTION WITH GRATITUDE AND LOVE, | Rumran

MANIFESTATION MINDSET: Why are you grateful to have this intention?

I am grateful to have good fortune because it allows me to live my life to the fullest and take care of my loved ones effortlessly.

(Get into the right mindset before you continue to write out the EXACT SAME manifestation intention from day 1 below)

1 I now draw good fortune my way, into every area of my reality.

2 I now draw good fortune my way, into every area of my reality.

3 I now draw good fortune my way, into every area of my reality.

4 I now draw good fortune my way, into every area of my reality.

5 I now draw good fortune my way, into every area of my reality.

6 I now draw good fortune my way, into every area of my reality.

7 I now draw good fortune my way, into every area of my reality.

8 I now draw good fortune my way, into every area of my reality.

9 I now draw good fortune my way, into every area of my reality.

10 I now draw good fortune my way, into every area of my reality.

11 I now draw good fortune my way, into every area of my reality.

12 I now draw good fortune my way, into every area of my reality.

13 I now draw good fortune my way, into every area of my reality.

14 I now draw good fortune my way, into every area of my reality.

15 I now draw good fortune my way, into every area of my reality.

16 I now draw good fortune my way, into every area of my reality.

17 I now draw good fortune my way, into every area of my reality.

18 I now draw good fortune my way, into every area of my reality.

19 I now draw good fortune my way, into every area of my reality.

20 I now draw good fortune my way, into every area of my reality.

21 I now draw good fortune my way, into every area of my reality.

22 I now draw good fortune my way, into every area of my reality.

23 I now draw good fortune my way, into every area of my reality.

24 I now draw good fortune my way, into every area of my reality.

25 I now draw good fortune my way, into every area of my reality.

26 I now draw good fortune my way, into every area of my reality.

27 I now draw good fortune my way, into every area of my reality.

28 I now draw good fortune my way, into every area of my reality.

29 I now draw good fortune my way, into every area of my reality.

30 I now draw good fortune my way, into every area of my reality.

31 I now draw good fortune my way, into every area of my reality.

32 I now draw good fortune my way, into every area of my reality.

33 I now draw good fortune my way, into every area of my reality.

I RELEASE MY INTENTION WITH GRATITUDE AND LOVE, Dawan

MANIFESTED INTENTION:

I now draw good fortune my way, into every area of my reality.

(REWRITE THE EXACT SAME manifestation intention from day 1 above)

MANIFESTATION SUCCESS STORY

Use these pages to write, illustrate or attach photos, receipts, evidence or proof of your 33x3 Success Story. This will help to document your manifesting journey and minimize resistence to future manifestations and the Law of Attraction.

33X3 CHALLENGE COMPLETION

MANIFESTATION INTENTION:

I am so grateful to be financially free.

(In the present tense & a place of gratitude, write a clear statement of your intended manifestation as if you already have it)

1 I am so grateful to be financially free.

2 I am so grateful to be financially free.

3 I am so grateful to be financially free.

4 I am so grateful to be financially free.

5 I am so grateful to be financially free.

6 I am so grateful to be financially free

7 I am so grateful to be financially free.

8 I am so grateful to be financially free.

9 I am so grateful to be financially free

10 I am so grateful to be financially free.

11 I am so grateful to be financially free.

12 I am so grateful to be financially free.

13 I am so grateful to be financially free.

14 I am so grateful to be financially free.

15 I am so grateful to be financially free.

16 I am so grateful to be financially free.

17 I am so grateful to be financially free.

18 I am so grateful to be financially free.

19 I am so grateful to be financially free.

20 I am so grateful to be financially free.

21 I am so grateful to be financially free.

22 I am so grateful to be financially free.

23 I am so grateful to be financially free.

24 I am so grateful to be financially free.

25 I am so grateful to be financially free.

26 I am so grateful to be financially free.

27 I am so grateful to be financially free.

28 I am so grateful to be financially free.

29 I am so grateful to be financially free.

30 I am so grateful to be financially free.

31 I am so grateful to be financially free.

32 I am so grateful to be financially free.

33 I am so grateful to be financially free.

I RELEASE MY INTENTION WITH GRATITUDE AND LOVE,

MANIFESTATION MINDSET: Why do you desire this intention in your life?

(Get into the right mindset before you continue to write out the EXACT SAME manifestation intention from day 1 below)

1

2

3

4

5

6

7

8

9

10

11

12

13

14

15

DAY 2

16

17

18

19

20

21

22

23

24

25

26

27

28

29

30

31

32

33

I RELEASE MY INTENTION WITH GRATITUDE AND LOVE,

MANIFESTATION MINDSET: Why are you grateful to have this intention?

(Get into the right mindset before you continue to write out the EXACT SAME manifestation intention from day 1 below)

1

2

3

4

5

6

7

8

9

10

11

12

13

14

15

16

17

18

19

20

21

22

23

24

25

26

27

28

29

30

31

32

33

I RELEASE MY INTENTION WITH GRATITUDE AND LOVE,

MANIFESTED INTENTION:

(REWRITE THE EXACT SAME manifestation intention from day 1 above)

MANIFESTATION SUCCESS STORY

Use these pages to write, illustrate or attach photos, receipts, evidence or proof of your 33x3 Success Story. This will help to document your manifesting journey and minimize resistence to future manifestations and the Law of Attraction.

MANIFESTATION INTENTION:

I have a $ 0.00 balance on my PC Financial Mastercard.

(In the present tense & a place of gratitude, write a clear statement of your intended manifestation as if you already have it)

1   I have a $0.00 balance on my

2

3

4

5

6

7

8

9

10

11

12

13

14

15

16

17

18

19

20

21

22

23

24

25

26

27

28

29

30

31

32

33

I RELEASE MY INTENTION WITH GRATITUDE AND LOVE,

MANIFESTATION MINDSET: Why do you desire this intention in your life?

(Get into the right mindset before you continue to write out the EXACT SAME manifestation intention from day 1 below)

1

2

3

4

5

6

7

8

9

10

11

12

13

14

15

16

17

18

19

20

21

22

23

24

25

26

27

28

29

30

31

32

33

I RELEASE MY INTENTION WITH GRATITUDE AND LOVE,

MANIFESTATION MINDSET: Why are you grateful to have this intention?

(Get into the right mindset before you continue to write out the EXACT SAME manifestation intention from day 1 below)

1

2

3

4

5

6

7

8

9

10

11

12

13

14

15

16

17

18

19

20

21

22

23

24

25

26

27

28

29

30

31

32

33

I RELEASE MY INTENTION WITH GRATITUDE AND LOVE,

MANIFESTED INTENTION:

(REWRITE THE EXACT SAME manifestation intention from day 1 above)

MANIFESTATION SUCCESS STORY

Use these pages to write, illustrate or attach photos, receipts, evidence or proof of your 33x3 Success Story. This will help to document your manifesting journey and minimize resistence to future manifestations and the Law of Attraction.

MANIFESTATION INTENTION:

I am so grateful that I have a $0.00 owing balance on my ~~P~~ PC Financial Mastercard.

(In the present tense & a place of gratitude, write a clear statement of your intended manifestation as if you already have it)

1 I am so grateful that I have a $0.00 owing balance on my PC Financial mastercard.

2 I am so grateful that I have a $0.00 owing balance on my PC Financial mastercard.

3 I am so grateful that I have a $0.00 owing balance on my PC Financial mastercard.

4 I am so grateful that I have a $0.00 owing balance on my PC Financial Mastercard.

5 I am so grateful that I have a $0.00 owing balance on my PC financial mastercard.

6 I am so grateful that I have a $0.00 owing balance on my PC financial mastercard.

7 I am so grateful that I have a $0.00 owing balance on my PC financial mastercard.

8 I am so grateful that I have a $0.00 owing balance on my PC financial mastercard.

9 I am so grateful that I have a $0.00 owing balance on my PC financial mastercard.

10 I am so grateful that I have a $0.00 owing balance on my PC financial mastercard.

11 I am so grateful that I have a $0.00 owing balance on my PC financial mastercard.

12 I am so grateful that I have a $0.00 owing balance on my PC financial mastercard.

13 I am so grateful that I have a $0.00 owing balance on my PC financial mastercard.

14 I am so grateful that I have a $0.00 owing balance on my PC financial mastercard.

15 I am so grateful that I have a $0.00 owing balance on my PC financial mastercard.

16 I am so grateful that I have a $0.00 owing balance on my PC financial mastercard.

17 I am so grateful that I have a $0.00 owing balance on my PC financial mastercard.

18 I am so grateful that I have a $0.00 owing balance on my PC financial mastercard.

19 I am so grateful that I have a $0.00 owing balance on my PC financial mastercard.

20 I am so grateful that I have a $0.00 owing balance on my PC financial mastercard.

21 I am so grateful that I have a $0.00 owing balance on my PC financial mastercard.

22 I am so grateful that I have a $0.00 owing balance on my PC financial mastercard.

23 I am so grateful that I have a $0.00 owing balance on my PC financial mastercard.

24 I am so grateful that I have a $0.00 owing balance on my PC financial mastercard.

25 I am so grateful that I have a $0.00 owing balance on my PC financial mastercard.

26 I am so grateful that I have a $0.00 owing balance on my PC financial mastercard.

27 I am so grateful that I have a $0.00 owing balance on my PC financial mastercard.

28 I am so grateful that I have a $0.00 owing balance on my PC financial mastercard.

29 I am so grateful that I have a $0.00 owing balance on my PC financial mastercard.

30 I am so grateful that I have a $0.00 owing balance on my PC financial mastercard.

31 I am so grateful that I have a $0.00 owing balance on my PC financial mastercard.

32 I am so grateful that I have a $0.00 owing balance on my PC financial mastercard.

33 I am so grateful that I have a $0.00 owing balance on my PC financial mastercard.

I RELEASE MY INTENTION WITH GRATITUDE AND LOVE,

MANIFESTATION MINDSET: Why do you desire this intention in your life?

(Get into the right mindset before you continue to write out the EXACT SAME manifestation intention from day 1 below)

1

2

3

4

5

6

7

8

9

10

11

12

13

14

15

16

17

18

19

20

21

22

23

24

25

26

27

28

29

30

31

32

33

I RELEASE MY INTENTION WITH GRATITUDE AND LOVE,

MANIFESTATION MINDSET: Why are you grateful to have this intention?

(Get into the right mindset before you continue to write out the EXACT SAME manifestation intention from day 1 below)

1

2

3

4

5

6

7

8

9

10

11

12

13

14

15

16

17

18

19

20

21

22

23

24

25

26

27

28

29

30

31

32

33

I RELEASE MY INTENTION WITH GRATITUDE AND LOVE,

MANIFESTED INTENTION:

(REWRITE THE EXACT SAME manifestation intention from day 1 above)

MANIFESTATION SUCCESS STORY

Use these pages to write, illustrate or attach photos, receipts, evidence or proof of your 33x3 Success Story. This will help to document your manifesting journey and minimize resistence to future manifestations and the Law of Attraction.

MANIFESTATION INTENTION:

(In the present tense & a place of gratitude, write a clear statement of your intended manifestation as if you already have it)

1

2

3

4

5

6

7

8

9

10

11

12

13

14

15

16

17

18

19

20

21

22

23

24

25

26

27

28

29

30

31

32

33

I RELEASE MY INTENTION WITH GRATITUDE AND LOVE,

MANIFESTATION MINDSET: Why do you desire this intention in your life?

(Get into the right mindset before you continue to write out the EXACT SAME manifestation intention from day 1 below)

1

2

3

4

5

6

7

8

9

10

11

12

13

14

15

16

17

18

19

20

21

22

23

24

25

26

27

28

29

30

31

32

33

I RELEASE MY INTENTION WITH GRATITUDE AND LOVE,

MANIFESTATION MINDSET: Why are you grateful to have this intention?

(Get into the right mindset before you continue to write out the EXACT SAME manifestation intention from day 1 below)

1

2

3

4

5

6

7

8

9

10

11

12

13

14

15

DAY 3

16

17

18

19

20

21

22

23

24

25

26

27

28

29

30

31

32

33

I RELEASE MY INTENTION WITH GRATITUDE AND LOVE,

MANIFESTED INTENTION:

(REWRITE THE EXACT SAME manifestation intention from day 1 above)

MANIFESTATION SUCCESS STORY

Use these pages to write, illustrate or attach photos, receipts, evidence or proof of your 33x3 Success Story. This will help to document your manifesting journey and minimize resistence to future manifestations and the Law of Attraction.

MANIFESTATION INTENTION:

(In the present tense & a place of gratitude, write a clear statement of your intended manifestation as if you already have it)

1

2

3

4

5

6

7

8

9

10

11

12

13

14

15

16

17

18

19

20

21

22

23

24

25

26

27

28

29

30

31

32

33

I RELEASE MY INTENTION WITH GRATITUDE AND LOVE,

MANIFESTATION MINDSET: Why do you desire this intention in your life?

(Get into the right mindset before you continue to write out the EXACT SAME manifestation intention from day 1 below)

1

2

3

4

5

6

7

8

9

10

11

12

13

14

15

16

17

18

19

20

21

22

23

24

25

26

27

28

29

30

31

32

33

I RELEASE MY INTENTION WITH GRATITUDE AND LOVE,

MANIFESTATION MINDSET: Why are you grateful to have this intention?

(Get into the right mindset before you continue to write out the EXACT SAME manifestation intention from day 1 below)

1

2

3

4

5

6

7

8

9

10

11

12

13

14

15

DAY 3

16

17

18

19

20

21

22

23

24

25

26

27

28

29

30

31

32

33

I RELEASE MY INTENTION WITH GRATITUDE AND LOVE,

MANIFESTED INTENTION:

(REWRITE THE EXACT SAME manifestation intention from day 1 above)

MANIFESTATION SUCCESS STORY

Use these pages to write, illustrate or attach photos, receipts, evidence or proof of your 33x3 Success Story. This will help to document your manifesting journey and minimize resistence to future manifestations and the Law of Attraction.

33X3 CHALLENGE COMPLETION

MANIFESTATION INTENTION:

(In the present tense & a place of gratitude, write a clear statement of your intended manifestation as if you already have it)

1

2

3

4

5

6

7

8

9

10

11

12

13

14

15

16

17

18

19

20

21

22

23

24

25

26

27

28

29

30

31

32

33

I RELEASE MY INTENTION WITH GRATITUDE AND LOVE,

MANIFESTATION MINDSET: Why do you desire this intention in your life?

(Get into the right mindset before you continue to write out the EXACT SAME manifestation intention from day 1 below)

1

2

3

4

5

6

7

8

9

10

11

12

13

14

15

16

17

18

19

20

21

22

23

24

25

26

27

28

29

30

31

32

33

I RELEASE MY INTENTION WITH GRATITUDE AND LOVE,

MANIFESTATION MINDSET: Why are you grateful to have this intention?

(Get into the right mindset before you continue to write out the EXACT SAME manifestation intention from day 1 below)

1

2

3

4

5

6

7

8

9

10

11

12

13

14

15

DAY 3

16

17

18

19

20

21

22

23

24

25

26

27

28

29

30

31

32

33

I RELEASE MY INTENTION WITH GRATITUDE AND LOVE,

MANIFESTED INTENTION:

(REWRITE THE EXACT SAME manifestation intention from day 1 above)

MANIFESTATION SUCCESS STORY

Use these pages to write, illustrate or attach photos, receipts, evidence or proof of your 33x3 Success Story. This will help to document your manifesting journey and minimize resistence to future manifestations and the Law of Attraction.

DATE ____ / ____ / ____   TIME ____ : ____ AM / PM

MANIFESTATION INTENTION:

(In the present tense & a place of gratitude, write a clear statement of your intended manifestation as if you already have it)

1

2

3

4

5

6

7

8

9

10

11

12

13

14

15

DAY 1

16

17

18

19

20

21

22

23

24

25

26

27

28

29

30

31

32

33

I RELEASE MY INTENTION WITH GRATITUDE AND LOVE,

MANIFESTATION MINDSET: Why do you desire this intention in your life?

(Get into the right mindset before you continue to write out the EXACT SAME manifestation intention from day 1 below)

1

2

3

4

5

6

7

8

9

10

11

12

13

14

15

16

17

18

19

20

21

22

23

24

25

26

27

28

29

30

31

32

33

I RELEASE MY INTENTION WITH GRATITUDE AND LOVE,

MANIFESTATION MINDSET: Why are you grateful to have this intention?

(Get into the right mindset before you continue to write out the EXACT SAME manifestation intention from day 1 below)

1

2

3

4

5

6

7

8

9

10

11

12

13

14

15

16

17

18

19

20

21

22

23

24

25

26

27

28

29

30

31

32

33

I RELEASE MY INTENTION WITH GRATITUDE AND LOVE,

MANIFESTED INTENTION:

(REWRITE THE EXACT SAME manifestation intention from day 1 above)

MANIFESTATION SUCCESS STORY

Use these pages to write, illustrate or attach photos, receipts, evidence or proof of your 33x3 Success Story. This will help to document your manifesting journey and minimize resistence to future manifestations and the Law of Attraction.

33X3 CHALLENGE COMPLETION

MANIFESTATION INTENTION:

(In the present tense & a place of gratitude, write a clear statement of your intended manifestation as if you already have it)

1

2

3

4

5

6

7

8

9

10

11

12

13

14

15

16

17

18

19

20

21

22

23

24

25

26

27

28

29

30

31

32

33

I RELEASE MY INTENTION WITH GRATITUDE AND LOVE,

MANIFESTATION MINDSET: Why do you desire this intention in your life?

(Get into the right mindset before you continue to write out the EXACT SAME manifestation intention from day 1 below)

1

2

3

4

5

6

7

8

9

10

11

12

13

14

15

DAY 2

16

17

18

19

20

21

22

23

24

25

26

27

28

29

30

31

32

33

I RELEASE MY INTENTION WITH GRATITUDE AND LOVE,

MANIFESTATION MINDSET: Why are you grateful to have this intention?

(Get into the right mindset before you continue to write out the EXACT SAME manifestation intention from day 1 below)

1

2

3

4

5

6

7

8

9

10

11

12

13

14

15

16

17

18

19

20

21

22

23

24

25

26

27

28

29

30

31

32

33

I RELEASE MY INTENTION WITH GRATITUDE AND LOVE,

MANIFESTED INTENTION:

(REWRITE THE EXACT SAME manifestation intention from day 1 above)

MANIFESTATION SUCCESS STORY

Use these pages to write, illustrate or attach photos, receipts, evidence or proof of your 33x3 Success Story. This will help to document your manifesting journey and minimize resistence to future manifestations and the Law of Attraction.

33X3 CHALLENGE COMPLETION

MANIFESTATION INTENTION:

(In the present tense & a place of gratitude, write a clear statement of your intended manifestation as if you already have it)

1

2

3

4

5

6

7

8

9

10

11

12

13

14

15

16

17

18

19

20

21

22

23

24

25

26

27

28

29

30

31

32

33

I RELEASE MY INTENTION WITH GRATITUDE AND LOVE,

MANIFESTATION MINDSET: Why do you desire this intention in your life?

(Get into the right mindset before you continue to write out the EXACT SAME manifestation intention from day 1 below)

1

2

3

4

5

6

7

8

9

10

11

12

13

14

15

16

17

18

19

20

21

22

23

24

25

26

27

28

29

30

31

32

33

I RELEASE MY INTENTION WITH GRATITUDE AND LOVE,

MANIFESTATION MINDSET: Why are you grateful to have this intention?

(Get into the right mindset before you continue to write out the EXACT SAME manifestation intention from day 1 below)

1

2

3

4

5

6

7

8

9

10

11

12

13

14

15

16

17

18

19

20

21

22

23

24

25

26

27

28

29

30

31

32

33

I RELEASE MY INTENTION WITH GRATITUDE AND LOVE,

33X3 CHALLENGE COMPLETED ON DATE ____/____/____ TIME ____:____ AM / PM

MANIFESTED INTENTION:

(REWRITE THE EXACT SAME manifestation intention from day 1 above)

MANIFESTATION SUCCESS STORY

Use these pages to write, illustrate or attach photos, receipts, evidence or proof of your 33x3 Success Story. This will help to document your manifesting journey and minimize resistence to future manifestations and the Law of Attraction.

33X3 CHALLENGE COMPLETION

MANIFESTATION INTENTION:

(In the present tense & a place of gratitude, write a clear statement of your intended manifestation as if you already have it)

1

2

3

4

5

6

7

8

9

10

11

12

13

14

15

16

17

18

19

20

21

22

23

24

25

26

27

28

29

30

31

32

33

I RELEASE MY INTENTION WITH GRATITUDE AND LOVE,

MANIFESTATION MINDSET: Why do you desire this intention in your life?

(Get into the right mindset before you continue to write out the EXACT SAME manifestation intention from day 1 below)

1

2

3

4

5

6

7

8

9

10

11

12

13

14

15

16

17

18

19

20

21

22

23

24

25

26

27

28

29

30

31

32

33

I RELEASE MY INTENTION WITH GRATITUDE AND LOVE,

DATE ____/____/____   TIME ____:____ AM / PM

MANIFESTATION MINDSET: Why are you grateful to have this intention?

(Get into the right mindset before you continue to write out the EXACT SAME manifestation intention from day 1 below)

1

2

3

4

5

6

7

8

9

10

11

12

13

14

15

16

17

18

19

20

21

22

23

24

25

26

27

28

29

30

31

32

33

I RELEASE MY INTENTION WITH GRATITUDE AND LOVE,

MANIFESTED INTENTION:

(REWRITE THE EXACT SAME manifestation intention from day 1 above)

MANIFESTATION SUCCESS STORY

Use these pages to write, illustrate or attach photos, receipts, evidence or proof of your 33x3 Success Story. This will help to document your manifesting journey and minimize resistence to future manifestations and the Law of Attraction.

33X3 CHALLENGE COMPLETION

MANIFESTATION INTENTION:

(In the present tense & a place of gratitude, write a clear statement of your intended manifestation as if you already have it)

1

2

3

4

5

6

7

8

9

10

11

12

13

14

15

16

17

18

19

20

21

22

23

24

25

26

27

28

29

30

31

32

33

I RELEASE MY INTENTION WITH GRATITUDE AND LOVE,

DATE ____/____/____   TIME ____:____ AM / PM

MANIFESTATION MINDSET: Why do you desire this intention in your life?

(Get into the right mindset before you continue to write out the EXACT SAME manifestation intention from day 1 below)

1
2
3
4
5
6
7
8
9
10
11
12
13
14
15

16

17

18

19

20

21

22

23

24

25

26

27

28

29

30

31

32

33

I RELEASE MY INTENTION WITH GRATITUDE AND LOVE,

MANIFESTATION MINDSET: Why are you grateful to have this intention?

(Get into the right mindset before you continue to write out the EXACT SAME manifestation intention from day 1 below)

1

2

3

4

5

6

7

8

9

10

11

12

13

14

15

DAY 3

16

17

18

19

20

21

22

23

24

25

26

27

28

29

30

31

32

33

I RELEASE MY INTENTION WITH GRATITUDE AND LOVE,

33X3 CHALLENGE COMPLETED ON DATE ____/____/____ TIME ____:____ AM / PM

MANIFESTED INTENTION:

(REWRITE THE EXACT SAME manifestation intention from day 1 above)

MANIFESTATION SUCCESS STORY

Use these pages to write, illustrate or attach photos, receipts, evidence or proof of your 33x3 Success Story. This will help to document your manifesting journey and minimize resistence to future manifestations and the Law of Attraction.

33X3 CHALLENGE COMPLETION

MANIFESTATION INTENTION:

(In the present tense & a place of gratitude, write a clear statement of your intended manifestation as if you already have it)

1

2

3

4

5

6

7

8

9

10

11

12

13

14

15

DAY 1

16

17

18

19

20

21

22

23

24

25

26

27

28

29

30

31

32

33

I RELEASE MY INTENTION WITH GRATITUDE AND LOVE,

MANIFESTATION MINDSET: Why do you desire this intention in your life?

(Get into the right mindset before you continue to write out the EXACT SAME manifestation intention from day 1 below)

1

2

3

4

5

6

7

8

9

10

11

12

13

14

15

16

17

18

19

20

21

22

23

24

25

26

27

28

29

30

31

32

33

I RELEASE MY INTENTION WITH GRATITUDE AND LOVE,

MANIFESTATION MINDSET: Why are you grateful to have this intention?

(Get into the right mindset before you continue to write out the EXACT SAME manifestation intention from day 1 below)

1

2

3

4

5

6

7

8

9

10

11

12

13

14

15

16

17

18

19

20

21

22

23

24

25

26

27

28

29

30

31

32

33

I RELEASE MY INTENTION WITH GRATITUDE AND LOVE,

`33X3 CHALLENGE COMPLETED ON` DATE _____/_____/_____   TIME _____:_____ AM / PM

MANIFESTED INTENTION:

(REWRITE THE EXACT SAME manifestation intention from day 1 above)

MANIFESTATION SUCCESS STORY

Use these pages to write, illustrate or attach photos, receipts, evidence or proof of your 33x3 Success Story. This will help to document your manifesting journey and minimize resistence to future manifestations and the Law of Attraction.

Manufactured by Amazon.ca
Bolton, ON

17887535R00067